THE DISCIPLINE OF SORROW.

" Toil, trial, and suffering, still await us, and the experience of every day teaches that we are not sufficient to ourselves.'

" Come unto me, all ye that are weary and heavy laden, and I will give you rest."

THE

DISCIPLINE OF SORROW.

BY

WILLIAM G. ELIOT,
Pastor of the Church of the Messiah, St. Louis.

They who sow in tears shall reap in joy.

FIFTH EDITION.

BOSTON:
WALKER, WISE, AND COMPANY,
PUBLISHERS FOR THE
AMERICAN UNITARIAN ASSOCIATION,
245 WASHINGTON STREET.
1863.

To

THE FAMILIES

AMONG WHOM I HAVE LIVED FOR MORE THAN TWENTY YEARS,
WHOSE SORROWS ARE MINE, AND WHOSE HEARTS
ANSWER TO MY OWN IN THE AFFECTIONATE
REMEMBRANCE OF OUR DEAD,

This Little Book

IS RESPECTFULLY DEDICATED BY THEIR FRIEND

W. G. E.

ADVERTISEMENT.

I AM almost tempted to hope that these pages will be read by none except those who have already learned, under the Discipline of Sorrow, that familiar truths bring the most effectual consolation. I have aimed at no originality of thought or novelty of expression, but, on the contrary, have sought to express the feelings which are common to all who mourn, in words which have become, through frequent use, the peculiar language of sorrow. To those who have felt only the lighter afflictions of life, the consolations here offered will seem trite and insufficient. But I humbly hope that those upon whom the heavier burden has been laid, and who do not seek diversion from grief, but the power of Christian endurance, will recognize in these common words their own individual experience, and perhaps be assisted in finding the strength which they individually need.

St. Louis, Mo., May 11, 1855.

CONTENTS.

Preparation.

A spirit still prepared,
  And armed with jealous care,
Forever standing on its guard,
  And watching unto prayer.

Let him remember the days of darkness; for they shall be many.

O Lord, our Heavenly Father, who hast safely brought us to the beginning of this day, defend us in the same with thy great power, and grant that this day we may not fall into any sin, neither run into any danger; but that all our doings, being ordered by thy governance, may be righteous in thy sight, through Jesus Christ our Lord.

PREPARATION.

WE are not unmindful of the blessings which God bestows; nor do we complain of the trials of life, as if they were too severe. Yet we cannot help feeling that life is oftentimes a discipline of sorrow. The Scripture gives only the needful warning when it teaches us to remember the days of darkness, for they shall be many. We need to remember them, and to be daily prepared for them; for they will surely come, the sad days of adversity, suffering, and bereavement. The common lot belongs to our common humanity; and when we feel most secure misfortune may be nearest — when we account ourselves strongest we may be leaning upon a broken reed. At the point where we think no defence required sorrow may gain entrance, and find us unprepared.

If it were a question only of prudence and wisdom, it would be different. Then, by directing our attention more closely to the defences and safeguards of life, we might hope to escape. But, although we may thus avoid many troubles, and greatly lessen the amount of trial, there are still exposures against which human wisdom cannot guard; there are misfortunes which baffle all human foresight; there are griefs directly of God's sending, and no man has yet lived who has not had reason to say that the days of darkness are many.

We should therefore be prepared for them; and, as we retreat to the cheerful fireside when the storms of winter are around us, so should we, with equal foresight, and in preparation for a greater need, provide inward stores of light and heat, of pleasant thoughts and memories, of pure affections, of childlike faith, of undying hope, of resignation and fortitude, of energy to do, and resolution to endure, whatever may be appointed as our part in life.

With this view, we would look to some of the sources of comfort from which the soul derives light in the days of darkness. We shall best know the preparation to be made when we have learned, from our own experience, or that of others, what are the consolations which give permanent and effectual strength. In the times of trouble a great deal of miserable comfort is given, and they who do not understand the depths of sorrow to which the heart may go down increase its suffering by their efforts to console.

There are chiefly three sources from which effectual and increasing comfort is derived, and which become more abundant, and impart more perfect peace, in proportion to the greatness of calamity under which we suffer. First, a clear conscience; secondly, the Christian faith; thirdly, the accustomed performance of duty.

First, a clear conscience — a conscience void of offence towards God and towards man. We speak, of course, in a human sense, and not of that absolute perfection which none of us attain, and for which it is almost arrogant to hope. We mean a life well spent, and the feeling of self-respect before men, and of humble, confiding hope before God, to which, by such a life, we are entitled. It gives the consciousness of inward strength, and a steadfastness of heart which nothing else can bestow. It enables us to feel that the calamity has come as discipline, and not as punishment. It arms us against the sting of misfortune, and assures us that, though cast down, we cannot be destroyed. But, in proportion as we remember wrong in our lives, we are weakened under the burden of sorrow. In proportion as we feel that we have not deserved God's blessings, their withdrawal causes additional pain. We may not accuse ourselves of fault in the particular case, yet, if we are conscious of general unfaithfulness, that our talents have been wasted that our time has been misspent, that worldly cares have been our principal care, that God has been absent from our thoughts, and his blessings enjoyed without thanksgiving or prayer, then the weight of adversity becomes heavier, and the soul sinks under it almost with the feeling of despair. Still more, if the memory of specific guilt is awakened, with feelings of shame or of self-contempt, the afflictions under which we labor will seem doubly great; and although there may be no connection between the wrong done and the suffering endured, we can scarcely help interpreting the one as the deserved punishment of the other. The heart is thus deprived of its natural strength, and troubled thoughts come to interfere with its consolations.

The commission of sin is a wrong done to the soul, far beyond our conception at the time when committed. It puts us on a lower grade of existence ; it subjects us to lower influences ; it spoils the serenity of our temper ; it makes us dependent upon outward circumstances for inward peace ; it separates us from God, and the dear communion of his Spirit ; it estranges us from Jesus Christ, and from all sympathy with the pure and good ; and altogether it makes us incompetent to understand the dealings of God toward us, either in his mercies or his chastisements. Every sin committed makes it more difficult to trust in God, or resign ourselves to his will. It changes the expression of his face from love to anger, because it disturbs the atmosphere of our thoughts and feelings through which he is seen.

But the pure in heart see God as he is In the enjoyment of his blessings they rejoice in his love; and when the days of darkness come, the light which shines from heaven is only the more beautiful because of the gloom which rests upon the earth.

This is therefore the first counsel to those who would be prepared for the severe trials of life. Avoid sin; shun every wrong action; stoop to no meanness; yield to no bad passion; indulge no sinful appetite; for every such deviation from right, though long forgotten, is recorded in the secret chambers of the memory, to be read, whether we will or no, when the days of darkness come. But let the life be given to works of usefulness, and let the laws of Christian morality be carefully observed; let continual effort be made to live as Jesus lived, who went about doing good, who did no sin, neither was guile found in his mouth ; and, although we cannot thereby avoid grief, and may need to pray, in agony of spirit, as Jesus prayed, that the cup of sorrow may pass from us, yet, having the consciousness that we have labored to do God's will, we shall still be able to say, as Jesus said, "Thy will, not ours, be done." Sorrow, when unmingled with remorse, may bruise, but it cannot break the heart ; and the smoking flax will not be quenched.

The second preparation for the days of darkness is Christian faith. We speak of it as a preparation, because, if we wait to seek for it until the darkness has already come, we are like those who were compelled to go and buy oil for their lamps, when their lamps were already needed tc be bright and burning. Religion must be familiar to our minds, the channel into which our thoughts naturally turn, or it will be an imperfect source of comfort to the stricken soul. If we have, then, to argue against objections, and persuade ourselves of the truth, when the mind needs repose, and the heart is waiting for the word of divine compassion, "peace, be still," our condition, though not hopeless, must be very sad. Adversity often has the effect of awakening men to the necessity of religious faith ; but the case of those is far better who have understood the necessity before the trial comes. They are like men who sleep in their armor, and who, at the first moment of alarm, are ready for the conflict. They may be suddenly surprised in the midst of perfect security, and aroused from the pleasant dreams of home and kindred to a contest of life and death. But their first conscious thought is that God is with them, and that he has already given the earnest of victory. " When we lie down to sleep thou art our defence, and when we awake we are still with thee." Such is the blessed influence of Christian faith upon all who heartily receive it, in preparing them for the severer conflicts of life.

We are not speaking of disputed questions in theology, but of the faith which is in common to all those who sincerely believe in Christ. It is to believe in the parental love and kind providence of God.. It is to believe that while we were yet sinners Christ died for us. It is to believe that earth is a place of discipline, where not only joy, but sorrow, is a proof of the divine goodness, and that whom God loveth he chasteneth. It is to hear the heavenly voice of Jesus, "Come unto me, all ye that are weary and heavy laden, and I will give you rest." It is faith in immortality, in redemption, and in the soul's communion with God. And, whatever else there may be which forms within us the life of Christ, and brings us near to the infinite God, his Father and our Father, and teaches us to count all things but loss for Christ's sake, while we press forward towards the mark for the prize of our high calling, this is what we mean by the Christian faith. It is the education of the soul in spiritual life; the rising above the world while we live in it, so that the clouds which cast a shadow upon our path can no longer obscure the upward vision. Life may be a baptism of sorrow, but by Christian faith we are baptized into the Holy Spirit. It confirms us amidst all doubts ; it allays our fears ; it speaks of pardon to the sinner, and of a blessing upon those who mourn. It tells us of the departed, that they are not dead, but sleeping. It reveals to the bereaved heart the mansions of the blessed, which Jesus has gone to prepare ; and, although it leaves us in a world of mystery, teaches us even here to trust. Ah ! how little do we know of the religion of Christ, until the days of darkness come!

Therefore, let those who would be prepared for all the vicissitudes of life, its disappointments, its bereavements, become earnest seekers of religion, until the Christian faith is the breath of their nostrils, the common air in which they live. Let them fill their hearts with it. Let it pervade their homes, and govern their families. Among all the realities of life let it be regarded, as it is, in fact, the chief reality. Thus having their daily walk with God, when they come to the dark valley of sorrow and of the shadow of death, his rod and his staff will comfort them. Earth has no sorrow which Heaven cannot heal.

Another source of returning strength in the time of adversity, and of consolation in bereavement, is found in the accustomed performance of duty. "Whatsoever thy hand findeth to do, do it with thy might," is sometimes the first word of practical comfort, and brings the earliest relief. The words of sympathy may be heard with patience, and will by and by be remembered with gratitude. The hearty encouragement of friends may arouse us from despondency, and prepare us for new exertion; but the heart's pulse cannot become healthy when the hands are idle. We must return to our working, and to the daily routine of life's duties, however cheerless the task may be, and however difficult. We may have no heart for it, and rather a feeling of weariness and disgust; but the exertion for duty's sake will be like medicine to the soul. The sooner we are compelled to receive it, the better for us; and the necessity of working, which seems at first a hardship, is found to be a blessing. It is therefore to be accounted one of the aggravations of severe affliction that it throws the mind off from its balance, and for the moment paralyzes its energies, so that the capacity of working is lost. Sometimes, too, a change is produced in our position, so that the ordinary routine of duty is stopped, and an interval of comparative idleness must be endured until the fierceness of the calamity be overpast. But the sooner we can return to accustomed duties, and the more exactly we perform them, the better. We may not do them heartily, but yet faithfully. If they are such duties as can be performed mechanically, while our thoughts are elsewhere, they will be the easier, and the less wearing to the mind. If they are such as to require hearty interest in them for their proper performance, it is probable that they will, at first, be imperfectly done, and the voluntary effort to do them may come very hard. But, whatever the case may be, no one ever gains by shrinking from his duty, and the continual effort should be made. Hour after hour will bring its own strength. One duty helps us on to another. The endeavor to serve God brings us nearer to him, and we submit to his divine will, not only with patience, but in that active coöperation by which we become instruments in his hands, and cheerfully go forward in the path which he has ordained, although it may lead through sorrow unto death. To sit down and weep, although we may say God's will be done, is not the Christian resignation. It is to arise from that prayer, with Jesus Christ, and go forward to the completion of our work.

It may be a hard lesson to learn, but it does not the less need to be taught. Until we have learned it, we are not strong to endure the heavy trials of life, and fail to derive from them their best instruction. He who is withdrawn from his duty by grief, and spends his time in the idleness of regret, is adding to the providential infliction the feeling of personal unfaithfulness, still harder to endure. If the calamity under which he suffers be worldly mortification and loss, let him grapple with the difficulty without complaint, and, by manly enterprise, correcting the faults of the past, command success for the future. If it be a heavier loss, for which earth has no healing, and time no cure, let us remember that the only road which leads to the heavenly physician is the path of duty, and, if we would be followers of Jesus Christ, we must also be the bearers of his cross.

We may perceive, therefore, the force of the words used, that the accustomed performance of duty is a source of consolation, and of renewed strength. We must have previous habits of industry, and the regular employment of time, or adversity will find us without nerve for exertion, and without energy of will. It is then no time to learn how to work, and how to forget one's self in the work done. Strictly voluntary exertion is almost impossible, and we need all the strength of former habit to enable us to act like men. But, if trouble finds us in the midst of our duties, the hands may continue to work; the mind, for a moment distracted, soon recovers its tone, and the heart, arousing from the first consternation of grief, is prepared, by obedience to the will of God, for the consolations of his Spirit. For we are then doing our part with faithfulness, and God will sustain and strengthen us. He shall come down like rain upon the mown grass, like dew upon the plant which perisheth ; for as a father pitieth his children, so doth the Lord pity those who fear him.

However severe the trials of life may be, we can therefore always hold ourselves in readiness for them. One word of counsel includes all. " Fear God and keep his commandments ; for this is the whole of manhood, the whole duty of man." Having a good conscience, putting our trust in God through Jesus Christ, living in the daily performance of our duty, and doing it as unto the Lord, we are prepared for every emergency of life, and under its severest trials the Comforter will be with us. " Peace I leave with you, my peace I give unto you," said the Saviour. " Let not your heart be troubled, neither let it be afraid."

Trial.

There is a battle to be fought,
An upward race to run,
A crown of glory to be sought,
A victory to be won.

With the baptism that I am baptized with, ye shall be baptized.

No chastening for the present seems joyous, but grievous; but afterward it yields the peaceable fruits of righteousness.

O God, who knowest us to be set in the midst of so many and great dangers, that by reason of the frailty of our nature we cannot always stand upright; grant to us such strength and protection as may support us in all dangers, and carry us through all temptations, through Jesus Christ our Lord.

TRIAL.

We do not seek, however, to conceal from ourselves the severity of discipline to which, under the providence of God, we are here subjected. It would not be difficult to give such representations of human life as would make it appear anything but a blessing. From some points of view it seems to be nothing but trouble and care, a weary progress of pain and disappointment, of vexation and loss. To say nothing of its sins and the retribution of sin, which are in themselves the worst evils, there is enough suffering from providential causes, over which we have little or no control, to fill our hearts with sad ness, and to make us feel as if we were walking in a gloomy path, which must become more and more gloomy to the end. An infancy of tears, a childhood of dis appointments, a youth of mistakes, a manhood of care, an old age of weariness and despondency, with its gray hair and tottering steps brought down in sorrow to the tomb. "Vanity of vanities," saith the preacher, "all is vanity."

First, there are the pains and bodily diseases, the thousand natural shocks that flesh is heir to. We may lessen them by temperance and careful obedience to the laws of health; but none of us can altogether escape. There will be many days and weeks in which we shall say we have no pleasure in them. In the morning we cry out, would God that it were evening, and when the night comes, would God that it were morning. Or, if the pain is not suffered in our own persons, we may have a harder trial in witnessing the pain of those whom we love, and who look to us for the relief which we are not able to give. Perhaps it is at the bedside of one too young or too helpless to express his wants and sufferings, and over whom we watch in the helpless agony of despair. Perhaps it is a long-continued contest with some incurable disease, which baffles all skill, and goes on with uninterrupted course to the end. But, in some form or other, the trial comes to every family and household. How many are there at this moment to whom, upon their beds of suffering, day brings no relief, and night brings no repose !

Then there are the disappointments

and losses to which all are subject. Poverty is not the worst evil; for a man may be very poor, and very contented. But when his daily exertions fail to bring him daily bread, when his best industry cannot provide clothing and education for his children, when the anxiety for the morrow is forced upon him in spite of all his faith, and to the destruction almost of hope itself, the physical evil of poverty becomes a greater spiritual evil, weighing down the mind, and sometimes debasing the character. The poverty of which the world is so full, and which we are daily called upon to relieve, is an evil of increasing magnitude; and, although we may not suffer from it ourselves, its presence among us is a cause of grief, and our inability to remove it becomes a personal hardship. It spoils our comfort to know that there are so many within our daily reach who are yet removed beyond our effectual sympathy. To live in the midst of suffering which we have no power to relieve, is to share in the suffering ourselves.

Sometimes it comes still nearer to us, if not by absolute want, yet by the losses and reverses of fortune to which the most prosperous are exposed. The best secured fortune may be lost, and they who are now living in affluence may find themselves next week looking for the means of support. All their plans of life are frustrated, the luxuries upon which they had learned to depend as needful comforts must be given up, their position in society is changed, and they must begin life over again, once more to go through its struggles and endure its buffets, at a time when they had thought themselves almost secure in the haven of retired competency and wealth. Riches take to themselves wings and fly away. There is no investment absolutely secure from loss, except of that which we have honorably used to good and honorable purpose. Nor is it only the loss of what we may have earned, but still more it is the mortification incident to the loss, and the long series of vexations and troubles which must follow. The misunderstandings, the unjust reproaches, the unavailing regrets that those whom we sought to serve have been made to suffer, the oppressive feeling of debt which we would gladly coin our blood to pay, and we know not how many other feelings most distressing to those who have the nicest sense of honor, are implied in those words which we speak so carelessly, and which describe a thing of daily occurrence, the reverses of fortune. The life which is marked by such vicissitudes, and in which such changes are continually to be feared, is too full of care to be a life of enjoyment.

But what are these losses of outward temporal blessings, which future industry may restore, and which will be remembered by and by with pleasantness, compared with the loss of our household treasures, our friends and kindred, to whom our hearts were given, and with whom our hearts are buried? How lonely and desolate is the house where bereavement has come! How heavy are the hearts of those who continue to do their appointed duties, which have now become a task-work, from which the relish has gone! How dreary is the path of life, with its miserable routine of cares, its childish toys and playthings, its amusements and its follies, to those who have looked upon the angel of death, and who have stood by the open grave! It is not that they would complain, but that they are bereaved. Rachel weeping for her children, and refusing to be comforted because they are not. Every family has its vacant seats at the fireside; every heart at times seeks for those who are living, in the places of the dead. We cannot escape the pains of bereavement; our dearest love cannot hold back those whom God calleth; and while we mourn for the departed, trembling mixes with our love for those who remain.

It is thus that the dread element of uncertainty is everywhere present, to lessen and often to spoil our best enjoyments. The danger of losing whatever we possess, and whatever we enjoy, is always impending; and the feeling of security is one which we can never wisely entertain. For, if it were possible to protect ourselves from pain and disease, if we could insure our possessions against the possibility of loss, if we could close our doors against that visitor who comes with equal tread to the threshold of rich and poor, and who chooses first those who are loveliest — if we could thus secure the permanence of all the conditions which belong to a prosperous life, yet does our own life itself continue only from day to day. We are but tenants at will, to be removed with or without warning. This night shall thy soul be required of thee; and then whose shall all those things be? The windows of the house are darkened, the wheel is broken at the cistern, the pitcher is broken at the fountain, the mourners go about the streets for a few days remembering us, and then the place which knew us shall know us no more forever.

The indisputable fact that we may die at any moment is of itself enough, humanly speaking, and with only a human view, to make the thought of happiness absurd. We must put it out of view, or human enjoyment is impossible. And therefore God has graciously ordained that, while we know and admit the fact whenever it is distinctly stated, it comes to us rather as an abstract proposition, a general law of humanity, than as a truth of personal application. Only by a strong mental effort does it come to the individual so as to be a personal concern.

It scarcely ever comes at all in the hours of happiness, and we live on from day to day with a feeling of security, although well knowing that we are not secure; and reach forward with our plans and schemings with a self-assured certainty of many years, when we know well enough that we ought not to count upon as many days. This is not mere thoughtlessness on our part, nor is it generally a wilful confidence in the duration of life. It is the wise and merciful ordering of Providence, without which the best provided life would be unhappy. If the uncertainty of life were ever present with us, dwelling in our thoughts, seen by the mind's eye, as the fact really is, not one of us could enjoy, and few could endure, to live. If we could see the arrows which fly by night, passing so near to us on every side a thousand thousand times before they touch us with their fatal point; if we could hear the silent tread of the pestilence which walketh in darkness, and the moving of its wings, which disturb the air we breathe, as it goes onward wasting at noonday; if we discerned the peril in which we thus continually stand, the dangers and the snares among which we so confidently move, our only prayer would be that death might come quickly, to release us from the pain, the trembling, and the fear. The terror would continually be increased in proportion to the greatness of our seeming bliss; and God, in his mercy, has therefore made it possible for us to be happy by the gift of unconsciousness, so that, without reasoning upon the subject and against reason, we enjoy the present, and look forward to the future with instinctive confidence. But, for a truly happy life, for the happiness which reasonable beings crave, something more than this instinctive evasion of the truth must be given. By shutting our eyes to the danger, the childish pleasure-seeking of life may continue; but when we put away childish things, and become mature in understanding, we need some higher law by which to live, and under which to enjoy.

The proposition with which we began will therefore remain undisputed, that human life may be represented so as to appear anything but a desirable gift. When we think of the cares and anxieties, the burdens and vexations, the weariness and the pains, the conflicts and defeats, the disappointments and losses, the estrangements of friendship and the desertions of love, the betrayals of confidence and the returns of evil for good, when we think how often the abundance of joy is thus suddenly changed to bitterness of grief, we must either, if we are rational beings, lie down in despair under a burden too heavy to be borne, or we must rise up with a new and better strength, to breathe an atmosphere more serene, and to live above the world while we live in it. As rational beings, we cannot close our eyes to that which reason and experience declare ; but, as spiritual beings, we may enter into the counsel of God, and learn from him what is the reality of life amidst all of its seemings, what is its real meaning amidst all its illusions, what are its substantial joys amidst all its disappointments, what is the fixed and glorious result of all its changes. It is for this purpose that we have turned our thoughts to that which may at first seem a sad and gloomy view of life; it is that we may pass, by the necessity of the case, by the demand of our nature, by the upward yearning of the soul, to that which is a thousand times more true, and ten thousand times more glorious.

The key of interpretation, by which that is made plain which would otherwise be mysterious, and that made bright which would otherwise be gloomy, is supplied by the knowledge of God's purpose concerning us, and our consequent faith in his providential care. Only when our will is in opposition to his do the uncertainties and calamities of life over-burden us. While we think of present enjoyment as the chief end, no explanation of life's manifold sorrows can be given.

Adversity is then an unmixed evil, and every day of grief an irretrievable loss But when we know that the enjoyments of life, however rich and abundant, are not the purpose of life, but are only incidental to its real uses, we begin to understand that the same love which gives may, by its continued and higher action, take away.

The child, looking at the fruit-tree when covered with beautiful and fragrant blossoms, supposes that beauty and fragrance are its ultimate end. He is disappointed when the blossoms fall, and the tree appears to him unsightly and useless. But when he learns that the fruit now begins to be formed, he changes his thought, and understands that the blossoms were but the superfluous adornings, which must pass away before the real uses of the tree can appear. And so it is with our life. Its childhood and youth are filled with delights, its advancing years are crowned with blessings, we are led by a gentle hand over green pastures and by the still waters, and our cup of gladness runneth over. Then, with childlike thought, we rejoice in the abundance of God's gifts, and if we thank him at all, it is for the enjoyment conferred, and not for the love from which it proceeds, and by which it may presently be withdrawn. We need to learn that the purpose of the tree is to bear fruit, not flowers; and that the wisdom and goodness of God may abound only the more at the time when the blossoms fall.

But our lives are not like the trees of this colder clime, which are quite shorn of their beauty before the fruit begins to appear, but rather like the orange and citron tree, on which new blossoms continually come, and successively give place to the forming fruit. So, in our mortal life, one delight after another disappears, giving place to that higher instruction which is the intended fruit. But new delights continue to bloom around us, so that, together with the sadness of increasing wisdom, the spring and the summer of the heart are continually renewed. But still the truth remains, that the fruit, and not the flower, is the ultimate end. What is the will of God concerning us? It is that we should become holy; that we should grow to the stature of Christian manhood; that, by the discipline of life, its mingled joys and sorrows, we may be educated for heaven. All present enjoyment and suffering are to be regarded chiefly in that view. They are good or evil, not according to their seeming, but as they minister to that end. The beauties and the glories of life, its purest enjoyments, its sweetest charms, are often only the flowers that must fall before the fruit appears. If their continuance hindered the fruit, would their continuance be a proof of God's love? We may weep while we answer, and feel that the glory has departed from our house; but still, if we are not wayward children, we shall consent to that which the Lord doeth that it is right.

Believe, therefore, in the wisdom of God. Consider his great purpose concerning us, and although our path may be sometimes rugged and steep, we shall perceive that it is the right path, and leading us in the right way. The uncertainties of life are a needful part of its discipline. The stolen treasure of earth turns our thoughts to the treasure in heaven, which neither moth nor rust doth corrupt, and which thieves do not break through to steal. The pains of the body remind us of its mortality, and awaken us to the higher life of the soul. Adversity, however stern in its coming, looks back upon us with a smiling face when its lessons have been learned ; and bereavement, with the hand which smites, points upward to the heaven where our angels dwell. "Ye shall drink," said the Saviour, "of my cup ; and with the baptism wherewith I am baptized, ye shall be baptized withal." And do we not, like those brave-hearted disciples of olden time, do we not consent to the baptism, although in the bitterness of tears? Do we love the body so much that we would not rather save the soul? Do we shrink from the cross, when our eyes are already fixed upon the crown?

Understand, therefore, the purpose of God concerning us, and we shall understand all the mysteries of life. If we can make his purpose our own, we shall be saved from a great part of its temptations. We shall smile at its outward losses, we shall endure with patience its heavier griefs, we shall learn by waiting to serve God, and by suffering to become strong. We do not say that we can thereby secure uninterrupted enjoyment; but we shall secure, amidst the severest storms of life, uninterrupted peace. We shall secure uninterrupted progress. We shall make our earthly life, with all its adversities, an uninterrupted blessing. Consent to this eternal truth, that the soul's salvation is the great end to be accomplished, and we shall perceive that God doeth all things well.

Weakness and Strength

Forgive the weakness I deplore,
   And let thy peace abound in me,
That I may trust myself no more,
   But wholly cast myself on thee.
O! let my Father's strength be mine,
   And my devoted life be thine!

But when he saw the winds and the sea boisterous, he was afraid.

Lord, increase our faith.

Hear my prayer, O God, and hide not thyself from my petition. Take heed unto me and hear me, how I mourn in my prayer and am troubled. My heart is disquieted within me, and the fear of death is fallen upon me. Fearfulness and trembling are come upon me, and an horrible dread hath overwhelmed me. And I said, O that I had wings like a dove, for then would I fly away and be at rest. I would make haste to escape from the stormy wind and tempest. But yet I will call upon God, and the Lord shall save me. O, cast thy burden upon the Lord, and he shall sustain thee, and shall not suffer the righteous to fall.

WEAKNESS AND STRENGTH.

When a difficult duty was made known to the disciples, they came to Jesus and said, Lord, increase our faith. It is the same prayer which we need continually to offer. We sometimes desire more knowledge, and complain that revelation has not instructed us more fully, and sometimes we ask for more evidence of its truth. We suffer our minds to become perplexed with difficult doctrines, or with what are called philosophical explanations, which darken what knowledge we possess, and then, if religion fails to exercise upon us the needful control, and to give the desired comfort, we impute the blame to the religion, instead of imputing it to ourselves. We need not more instruction nor clearer evidence of the truth, but more faith. We need greater capacity of believing, and a more childlike spirit in its exercise.

Certainly our religion contains all the instruction that we need. It is adapted to all the exigences of life, and can supply all its wants. As a system of theology, it reveals God in his infinite perfections, so that we can understand his dealings with us ; and as a system of moral instruction, it develops all that is true in our nature. The heavenly Father, whom Christ makes known, is a being of infinite wisdom and of perfect goodness. His power is directed by love, and under his protection we are shielded from all harm. Among all the changes of life we may feel secure, because without him not even a sparrow falleth to the ground. By knowing his purposes concerning us, our redemption from sin, and the education of our souls for immortal life, the mysteries of his providence, otherwise inscrutable, receive explanation, and we can rest assured that while infinite wisdom directs, infinite power can execute the plans of infinite love, so that all things will ultimately work together for our good. Even the great mystery of sin is partly explained by the efficacy of repentance, and the promised reconciliation with God through Jesus Christ. Temptation is disarmed of its power to those who believe that God answers their prayers, and will find a way for their escape. The burdens of life become light to those who are supported by a divine arm. Adversity loses its threatening aspect, and becomes a proof of parental love. Bereavement, however sad, no longer leaves us to sorrow as those who have no hope; for the dead may yet belong to us not less, yea, even more than the living. Death itself is changed from an enemy to a friend, from a destroyer to a deliverer, by him who hath given us the victory. We are travellers through the wilderness to the promised land; we are children, receiving our education for the maturity of a nobler life; we are soldiers in the army of God, who must endure the conflict before the victory is gained; and, however dark the road may sometimes be, and however hard the lessons to be learned, and however fierce the battle in which we must engage, the pillar of cloud and fire still goes before us to guide, the voice of our heavenly teacher still encourages us to learn, and the armor of our God still defends us from harm. "Nothing," said the Saviour, "can, by any means, hurt you." Such are the words that he continually speaks. Seeming evil is real good. They who sow in tears shall reap in joy. Death opens the way to life, and the afflictions of the present time, which are but for a moment, are working out for us a far more exceeding, even an eternal weight of glory.

The instruction, therefore, is sufficient to those who receive it. We may multiply all the calamities of life beyond what any one has ever endured, and beyond what human strength can endure, until all human hope is gone, and all earthly joy departed ; and still the support given by our religion is sufficient for our need, the way of deliverance is still open, and the light from heaven shines continually brighter.

So at least it may be, and was intended to be. But how is it with us in fact? With the knowledge of God's love and paternal care, with the knowledge that Christ died for us and ever liveth to make intercession for us, with the knowledge that death is but the passing from an earthly to a heavenly home, with the knowledge that all our trials here are sent for our good, and that God is never manifesting his love more perfectly than when his hand of chastening is laid upon us, — with such instruction given to us by Christ, and received by us as true, what are our real feelings when calamity impends? How do we endure the chastisement? How do we actually receive the sterner discipline of life? The instruction is immediately forgotten, the explanations of God's providence no longer satisfy us, the purposes of God concerning us are disregarded, the promises of Christ seem to be afar off, the waves of sorrow go over us, and the light of God's presence is shut out from our souls. The disappointments and losses which come in the ordinary course of life are beyond our patient endurance, and the bereavements which make our homes desolate prostrate us almost in hopeless despair. Because one blessing has been taken away, there seems to be none left. Because there is one calamity, there seems to be no joy. Everything seems wrong, and, like the unfaithful prophet, when the vine withers and the sun beats down upon our heads, we say, and, what is still more, we feel, that it is better to die than to live. Trouble comes upon us, and we faint; it touches us, and we know not what to do. Where, then, is our fear, our confidence, the uprightness of our ways, and our hope?

It is not because we deliberately rebel against God, nor would we dare to take the ordering of our days out of his hands; but we are astounded, and know not which way to turn. It is not that we openly complain; but we shrink from the chastisement, and are unable to look up. Our minds tell us a thousand reasons why we should be comforted, but no word of comfort reaches the heart. What, then, is the difficulty? There must be some defect, some short-coming, some deficiency, or we could not be thus unfaithful and inconsistent. We may say that the spirit is willing and the flesh is weak, and that this is an explanation of the perpetual conflict and the occasional defeat. It is so. But why should that weakness continue? Why does not the spirit conquer? Why is the weakness of the body transferred to the soul, instead of the soul's strength transferred to the body? It is because our souls themselves are weak through the want of faith. Religion becomes an insufficient support, because it is not thoroughly believed. There may be no deliberate or intentional doubting, but there are involuntary misgivings and fears. The heart wavers, and the mind wavers with it. We had thought ourselves thoroughly convinced, but now we ask, almost with trembling, can it be true that God lives, does his providence never fail, in judgment does he remember mercy, is that which the Lord doeth always right?

We wonder at ourselves when such thoughts come. We are ashamed of the state of mind into which trouble has thrown us, and cannot understand it; yet it continues, and our souls are cast down within us. They are also sorely vexed, and even our prayer is that of despondency — O Lord, how long!

Shall we say that this is the condition of none but a worldly and irreligious man? That the Christian believer can never suffer from such misgivings, and weakness, and fears? But it is in the language of David that we have been speaking, and Paul himself, although ready to be offered up, exclaimed, "In this tabernacle of the flesh we do groan, being burdened." It is an experience through which every one, sooner or later, must pass; and spiritual strength is gained only by the knowledge and confession of weakness.

But what, then, shall we do? When these times of despondency overtake us, and we learn that we are still weak, even wherein we had thought ourselves strongest, how shall we find strength and comfort? Shall we argue over again each point of doctrine, and reëstablish every truth? No; for at such times the intellect does not lead the heart, but the heart leads the intellect. Shall we accuse ourselves of sin, as if all our former religion had been hypocrisy, and all our faith a delusion and lie? No; for our former religion was sincere, and our faith had proved equal to the former exigences of life. But under the heavier burden more strength is needed, and the severer trial has come that a higher lesson may be learned. From God alone can the needful strength be given; and we who are anxious, but scarcely able to believe, turn to him, as the apostles came to Jesus, with the prayer, "Increase our faith." Here is the difficulty, and here is the means of help. Increase our faith. Give to the spirit victory over the flesh. Enable us firmly to believe that which we now imperfectly discern to be true. Make the spiritual life real to us, so that we may walk by faith, and not by sight. Strengthen the belief of the intellect, and exalt it until it becomes the conviction of the whole soul. Bring heaven nearer to us, and make the presence of God so real that in him we may live, and move, and have our being. Bring eternity near, until death shall seem to us, as it is, the birth and starting-place of the soul. Lord, increase our faith!

But do we understand the full meaning of that prayer? It is not to increase our willingness to believe, for we are never more willing than when the greatness of calamity oppresses the soul. We are willing, nay, anxious to believe; but the confusion of our thoughts for the time prevails, and our hearts are disquieted within us. Nor is it chiefly to pray that the truth, partially revealed, should be more fully manifested. It is rather to pray that our whole capacity, as intellectual and moral beings, may be enlarged; that we may be lifted up from one grade of spiritual existence to another; that our nature itself may be exalted and purified. The things to be seen remain unchanged, but our eyes need to be opened. Open thou the eyes of my mind, that I may clearly discern the things which are in thy law!

The truths of religion are of such a kind that they become plainer to us as we advance in purity and goodness. Our real faith in God can be increased only by our becoming more like God. Unless we have the spirit of Christ, we are none of his. But, as the mists of sin are dispelled, which are the clouds obscuring God's countenance, we rise to a clearer light, we breathe with a larger inspiration, we live in a more glorious companionship. Our faith cannot be increased while we remain upon the same level. In proportion as we do his will, we know of his doctrine. We must come nearer to Christ to know him better, and only by becoming more pure in heart can we more clearly see our God. To pray for an increase of faith must therefore be accompanied by the prayer and by the exertion to become better men. But what do we say? It is but one and the same prayer, differently expressed; it is the same yearning of the soul towards the infinite and all-merciful God.

These are the words of truth and soberness. They are the fact of Christian experience in every human soul. As we become better, the mysteries of God's providence are explained. As our nature is exalted, the difficulties of Christian faith disappear. Do your duty twice as well, and your faith will be twice as strong. Conform your lives more perfectly to the will of God, and his dealings with you will become continually more plain. By thus having faith, although as a grain of mustard-seed, we shall be able to remove the most threatening obstacles from our path, the heaviest mountains of sorrow from our souls.

This is, therefore, the great lesson which we have to learn, and we should diligently seek to understand it. We acknowledge that our faith needs to be increased. It must be increased for our endurance of the discipline of life, which is sometimes so stern; for our resignation to its griefs and disappointments, which are sometimes so hard to bear. But the increase of faith is the enlargement of capacity. It is the manly growth of the soul. It is advancement in goodness. It is the renewal of the image of God. Therefore, in seeking for faith and praying for it, seek for this spiritual growth and pray for it. Once more we say that it is one and the same seeking, it is one and the same prayer.

How differently would the present life appear to us, if we were what we ought to be! If the conflict with sin had ceased, and the lesson of self-control were well learned. If our passions were all calmed, and our desires all pure. If no duty were deferred or neglected, and no purpose of wrong indulged. Where would then be the conflict of mind, the misgiving, and the doubt? Where would then be the mystery of God's providence, and the despairing loneliness of our hearts? Sorrow might still be the portion of our cup, and before its coming we might, for the moment, still pray that it should pass from us; but God's own angels would be near to comfort, and the peace which passeth all understanding would be ours.

May God therefore increase our faith! By becoming like Jesus Christ, may we learn to pray in his name. By being reconciled with God in the daily conduct of our lives, may we learn to be reconciled to his will. May our souls be so enlarged, and our hearts so purified from sin, that we may discern things as they are, and daily become more strong. May we thus rise above the seemings and illusions of the world, to dwell in the perfect truth of righteousness. Who shall grieve at that which is bringing him nearer to God? Lord, increase our faith!

Compensations.

Deem not that they are blessed alone
  Whose days a peaceful tenor keep;
The God who loves our race has shown
  A blessing for the eyes that weep.

It is better to go to the house of mourning than to the house of feasting; for the living shall lay it to heart.

Blessed are they that mourn; for they shall be comforted.

Most gracious and merciful Father, we resign ourselves and all our interests to thy disposal, in the humble hope that thy mercy will never forsake us, and that thou wilt cause all things to work together for our good. We would submit patiently to thy will under every affliction ; and we humbly pray that we may so pass through the changes of this world, as finally to be prepared for the enjoyment of perfect and eternal happiness in the world to come, through Jesus Christ our Lord.

COMPENSATIONS.

WE may thus learn to reconcile our selves to the will of God, under all afflictions, and to resign ourselves, without complaining, to the divine disposal. Every step of advancement in the Christian character adds to our Christian faith, until we learn to lay aside all doubt and fear, and to receive both joy and sorrow as equally proofs of parental love. When roused from the sweetest dreams of earthly bliss by that which seems to be the voice of warning and rebuke, we shall answer, "Speak, Lord, for thy servant heareth;" and although with tears in our eyes, and natural sadness in our hearts, renewedly commend ourselves to God, as unto a faithful Creator. We return again to the ordinary duties of life, believing that, although our human hopes are disappointed, we do not labor in vain in the Lord.

There is, however, a still higher and progressive experience, by which we may understand more perfectly the blessing pronounced upon those who mourn. It is the experience by which we are taught the compensations given, even here, to those upon whom the burden of grief is laid. The Scripture teaches that they who sow in tears shall reap in joy. And again, it is better to go to the house of mourning than to the house of feasting, for that is the end of all, and the living shall lay it to their hearts. They are words which we may have read and heard a thousand times, without thinking of them as being literally true. We have thought of them, perhaps, as belonging to the church and the pulpit, and as being true in some technical, religious sense, rather than as expressing the actual facts in the real experience of life. Or, if we have allowed to them an exact meaning, it has been only with reference to preparation for the future life. We have learned, perhaps, by observing the effect of adversity upon others and upon ourselves, that the trials of life are well calculated to purify and elevate the soul. But the present compensations of sorrow are not so easily discerned. We do not so willingly learn that even here, in the human relationships of life, of friends and kindred and home, it is possible for us to become the gainers by that which seems to be the greatest loss. That our real happiness in loving each other may be increased, and our whole life become more blessed in company with those whom we love, because of the shadows and the darkness in which we may have been appointed, for a time, to dwell. Nay, our hearts almost shrink from the suggestion of such a possible result, as if it implied forgetfulness of the dead.

Bereavement is indeed the deepest sorrow, in comparison with which all other providential griefs are easily endured. It is an absolute loss, for the place of those taken from us can never be supplied. It is a wound which cannot be perfectly healed, and the memory of the dead must always remain as an experience of continued sorrow. Yet as time, the consoler, bears us onward, and brings us continually nearer to those whose memory is so precious, their cherished forms become more and more beautiful, they seem to hover around us clothed in garments of angelic light, their faces beam with heavenly expression, and their dear remembered voices fill our ears with heavenly music. Our present communion with them has indeed ceased; for it could not continue consistently with the health of our minds, or without impairing the practical usefulness of this earthly life. It is not appointed to us to live in the body and out of the body at the same time. Even the communion of God's Spirit is granted to us only under such conditions that we cannot distinctly separate it from what we call the natural working of our own minds; nor can we say of it, "Lo! here, or lo! there," unless we claim to be expressly the inspired prophets of God. And so of the departed ones, who live in all our thoughts, and whose love consecrates all our affections. To our mortal sight and hearing they cannot return, and neither for their sake or our own should we desire it. Yet we may feel that they are still ours, not only to be remembered, but to be loved and cherished. For, although dead, they are yet living, and they still belong to us, our heavenly kindred, although the quiet earth has received their forms, and the place which once knew them can know them no more.

The memory of the dead! What is this life in comparison? What is there so real to us, so unchangeably real, as the memory of those true and faithful hearts which once beat with ours here, pulse for pulse, with whom we sorrowed and rejoiced, and who have gone before us, only a few steps in advance, cheering us, by the remembrance of their virtues, on the way to heaven! Tears may suffuse our eyes when we think of them, yet our thoughts of them are the indispensable treasure of the soul. To our mind's eye they continually return, taking their wonted places, greeting us with the kindly smile, and our ears are again filled with the sweet tones of their gentle voices. Time passes; the months and years roll on; the burdens of life are taken up and laid down; the cares of life vex us, and are forgotten; new joys and new sorrows intervene; new hopes and new disappointments exercise our affections; gray hairs begin to cover our heads ; the lines of thought deepen, until they become the wrinkles of old age ; but does the memory of the dead fade away ? Is our perception of the loss sustained less keen, or do they become to us as though they had never been ?

When we review the experience of our own trials, or enter into the experience of others by sympathy with their grief, we know that there is but one answer. The pain of bereavement is an abiding grief, and a portion of our own hearts and of our own lives belongs to the dead. It is indeed an irreparable loss that we have sustained, and we cannot hope again to be the same persons that we once were. The world is changed to us ; our position in it is changed ; its uses and purposes are no longer the same, and can never again appear in their former light. The household to which the angel of death has come can never forget his coming. The shadow which his wings have cast over the soul must remain, however clearly the light from God's own love may shine. Yes, when we are most perfectly resigned to his will, and most perfectly consoled under the loss by the dear promises of Christ, and most happy in the sweet hope of reünion with the dead, and most faithful in using the discipline which we know to be for our own good, the loss, in itself considered, may then seem, as it perhaps then becomes, greater than it ever was before. By the completeness of spiritual experience is the depth of our sorrow revealed. By the spiritual development of our affections the sacredness of earthly affection and of earthly relations is first discerned. A part of the blessing upon those who mourn comes by learning the greatness of their loss.

It is not, therefore, that time dulls our perceptions, or that the bereavement seems to be less. Religion does, indeed, console; but no part of the consolation is found in forgetfulness. Perhaps we may say with truth that the bereaved heart would not consent to the direct lessening of its grief, for it would imply a feebler consciousness of the treasure once possessed. We would not cease to mourn even when we most desire to be comforted.

But still may we not ask ourselves, with sadness of heart, indeed, but yet in the soberness of deliberate thought, — measuring the value of things according to their real worth, — would it have been better for us to keep all here? If all who began life with us had continued with us, if we had not known in our families what death means, would our sum of happiness have been increased? Would our present perception of God's goodness have been clearer? Would the real uses of life have been more fully accomplished?

They have gone from us, I know, and their loss can never be made good; but their having been here; the privilege that we enjoyed in knowing and loving them; the belief that those whom we love, and who love us in return, are in heaven; the sense of security in which we dwell for the departed, knowing as we do that their earthly trial is ended, and that the problem of mortal life has to them found a true solution; the feeling of personal connection with heaven and heavenly things by reason of the family ties which are extended there, — all this, although expressed imperfectly, and perhaps not distinctly perceived, yet, as a real experience, daily becoming more familiar to the bereaved heart, becomes a compensation infinitely precious, and may teach us, if we are willing to learn, that it is sometimes better to dwell in the house of mourning than in the house of feasting.

We do not say that it seems better, for the seeming is not always the truth. At the time when affliction is laid upon us, we are sometimes too deeply troubled to think soberly as we ought to think. We can see a thousand reasons why the cherished one should live : not one reason why he should die. It may be impossible at the time to discern wherein we are to be the gainers, under the sense of such real and oppressive loss. We are not speaking now of what may seem to us, but of what really is. The Scripture itself does not say that it seems better to go to the house of mourning, but that it *is* better. As a matter of fact, as our own real inward experience, if we have had any experience that can be called inward, we also may learn to say that it is better.

The best part of our experience is not enjoyment, but suffering. Our highest happiness comes not with laughter, but through tears. There are those who live only on the surface of life, whose hearts strike no roots deeper than the thin surface-soil which every passing storm washes or drives away, and leaves an unfruitful earthy clay beneath; and such persons, who live to eat and drink and be merry, may have no knowledge, and may desire no knowledge, of what we are now saying. To them the house of mourning is the house of mourning and nothing else. They shun it as a pestilence, and have nothing to learn there which their selfish and worldly nature is capable of learning. Pleasure and happiness are to them words of the same meaning; suffering and evil are but the same idea. It is not for them, nor to them, that we speak. We speak to those who have gone down into the depth of sorrow, but even there have been able to cry out unto the living God. We speak to those who are at least prepared to understand that the baptism of tears may be that which fits us for the baptism of the Holy Spirit.

We ask, therefore, appealing to our own experience and to theirs, whether we cannot distinctly trace a great part of what is noblest and best to what we have suffered. Has it been the prosperity or the adversity of life which has ministered most truly to our manliness of thought, to our love of virtue, to our capacity of real enjoyment? Let us take this question with us in the retrospect of the last ten years, for example, and try the good and evil of life by this practical test. Out of that experience could we now best afford to lose the working of our joys or of our sorrows? Has pleasure or pain done the most for us? Has the house of mourning or the house of feasting taught us the most? From what source have our noblest thoughts come? How have the purest affections been cultivated? If we are conscious that our love of virtue is stronger than it was, and that we are learning to live more habitually in the divine presence, have we learned it in the time of vigorous health, or upon the bed of sickness? Has God ever seemed so near to us as in the chamber of death? Has eternity ever been so real as when we have returned from standing at the open grave? Could we have known how much we loved those whom God had given, unless He had taken them away? Could we love those who are left with the same disinterested, prayerful, religious affection that we now feel, if we had not been taught to love them for eternity as well as for the present world?

We think that these questions lead us to a true answer. Our hearts may struggle against it, because of their weakness; but our profoundest experience teaches its truth. There is almost no really valuable experience, almost no enduring and real good, which does not come through the ministry of pain and suffering. The cross which we bear is that which raises us to heaven.

We have seen a family dwelling under the light of unclouded prosperity, where the radiance of Christian love has also been found. They have rejoiced together in the enjoyment of God's gifts, without forgetting to thank him as the giver. They have understood, so far as possible, the greatness of their blessings in remaining together a whole family, and a part of their daily prayer has been that they might always be spared the pain of bereavement. It would seem that they did not need the hand of chastisement, or the discipline of suffering, either to confirm their mutual love, or to bring them nearer to

God. And yet, even in a Christian family like this, when death has entered there, and some one of the dear household has been taken, it has proved to be a new revelation of God, and of their Saviour, and of their own hearts, to themselves. In all their religion they had not known before how completely man depends upon God. They had not known how absolutely essential to the human soul is the thought of the divine presence. They had not understood either the words or the character of Jesus. They had not known the depth of their own souls, nor the strength of their own affections. That one new experience has made all things new. The spiritual nature, although before recognized, now first appears in its true dignity, and for the first time they thoroughly understand that the real use of the present world is to educate the soul for heaven. They loved each other before, but new tenderness is now added to their love. Their kindness becomes more thoughtful, their affection more disinter ested. They feel their dependence upon each other more deeply, and watch over each other with silent, inexpressible love.

The fond union of youthful hearts seems very close, and causes them to dwell in an elysium of joy; but the husband and wife seldom know how much they love each other until they mourn together, weeping for their children because they are not.

How quickly are the little dissensions and variances of life stilled by the presence of death! How sternly is selfishness rebuked, and with what yearning of the heart towards Heaven is the resolution made to become more tender, more affectionate, more gentle, and more faithful in the whole conduct of life!

Such is the natural influence of sorrow shared in common. Hearts which rejoice cannot come so near to each other as hearts which grieve. Tears mingle more perfectly than smiles, and the chain of family love on earth becomes much stronger when some of its links are in heaven.

If this be true, the house of mourning may be better than the house of feasting, and they who sow in tears may reap in joy. Not only as a preparation for the future, but even in this world, our sum of happiness may be increased by sorrow. We do not speak ignorantly nor coldly, nor as those who never felt the agony of bereavement. We know what it is to look upon the dying child, and to watch over the parent's failing strength. We know how deep the grave seems when open to receive those whom we love. But we also know that in the severest grief we bear, if we hold to our Christian faith and continue in the performance of our duty, we are coming nearer to God, nearer to him who suffered on the cross, nearer to those who live, nearer to those who die. Except the grain of corn fall into the ground and die, it cannot spring forth into life. And until these poor human hearts have been buried under grief, their best affections cannot be developed in their divinest strength.

It is true, therefore, that our real happiness may become greater by its seeming diminution. We say it with hesitation, and almost with trembling ; yet it is true.

It is true, not only as an abstract proposi tion, but as a practical experience. Not by the number of our blessings, nor by their greatness, but by our capacity of enjoying them, is our daily happiness to be measured. If you would make men contented with their lot, the better plan sometimes is not to increase, but to diminish their store. They are discontented because they have too much. Take away one half, and they will learn to enjoy the rest better than they had ever enjoyed the whole. Cheerfulness of heart is often promoted by lessening the outward sources of delight, and compelling the heart to be the source of cheerfulness to itself. If we were required to name, among all whom we have known, those who have retained the most perfect cheerfulness and sweetness of temper, we should probably name some whose lives have been the continued experience of pain and suffering. Let there be Christian faith as the foundation, and in almost any given case, if our object were to train a human soul to habitual contentment and cheerfulness, and therefore to the enjoyment of life, the better course would be to place it under the discipline, not of unvaried prosperity, but of frequent pain and loss, and sometimes of severe suffering and bereavement. It is one of the sublime mysteries of the soul, that out of weakness we are thus made strong, that out of darkness springs forth the light.

Why, then, should we shrink from sorrow as if it were calamity? Why should the house of mourning be to us the house of misery and despair? We know that there is an instinctive love of enjoyment and ease. Laughter seems pleasantest, and joy is most attractive. It would be unnatural and hypocritical to say that we desire affliction; and it is right to avoid sorrow and loss whenever we can do so in the strict performance of our duty. To court misfortune, or foolishly to incur loss, would prevent the instruction which should come from the discipline of life. The feeling that we have done our best to avert calamity is needful to the efficacy of the trial. And so it is written of the Saviour himself, that he prayed, "If it be possible, let this cup pass from me;" and then added, "If it may not pass from me unless I drink it, thy will, not mine, be done." But, to avoid sorrow by the use of proper and just means, and to pray for our deliverance from it, is a very different thing from that dread of sorrow, that shrinking from it as if it were an absolute evil, which is unchristian distrust in God. However stern affliction may seem in its first coming, it soon wears a reconciling face, and whispers a benediction to the believing heart. We may feel the burden that we bear, and for a time bend under its oppressive weight, but still be daily learning the infinite truth, which changes earth to heaven, that all things work together for the good of those who love God.

Of those who love God. Let these words be observed, for they contain, not only encouragement, but also warning. The discipline of life is not compulsion, but discipline. Only to him who asks shall it be given. Prosperity does not always harden, affliction does not always soften, the heart. The sorrow which God sends is intended to make us pure, to exalt, to strengthen, to ennoble us. But we may turn it to the gall of bitterness, and, instead of purifying, it may burn the heart, and harden it in selfish grief. There is no possible discipline under which we can be compelled into goodness. Our work cannot be done for us, and the outward circumstances of life, whether of joy or sorrow, can minister to the soul only according to our willingness, under the grace of God, to be instructed. We need, therefore, in the time of prosperity, and before grief has entered in, to recognize the love of God in the blessings he bestows, in order to understand it in their removal. Thus would our enjoyment be doubly blest, and the severest grief would find its consolation.

The discipline is therefore of God's appointing, but its use, for good or evil, is our own. To-day we dwell in the house of feasting; to-morrow, in the house of mourning. That is not for us, but for God, to determine. But, under God, it is for us to say whether it shall be better for us, according to the Scripture, or not. Sorrow is almost sure to come. We cannot, and hereafter we shall thank God that we cannot, avoid it. Receive it as the discipline of parental love, and it will, at the same time, enlarge the happiness of earth, and smooth the way to heaven. The blessing upon those who mourn is a real benediction, and the alleviations of sorrow become a heavenly compensation.

Why, then, art thou cast down, O my soul, and why art thou disquieted within me? Hope thou in God; for I shall yet praise him who is the health of my countenance and my God.

For thou hast dealt well with thy servant, O Lord, according to thy promise. Before I was afflicted I went astray; but now have I kept thy word. Thou art good, and doest good; O, teach me thy statutes! It is good for me that I have been afflicted, that I might learn thy law. I have seen an end of all perfection, but thy commandment is exceeding broad.

www.ingramcontent.com/pod-product-compliance
Lightning Source LLC
LaVergne TN
LVHW021429110826
845150LV00007B/2154